Motorbooks International

MIL-TECH SERIES

HUMMER

M000248315

Michael Green

Motorbooks International
Publishers & Wholesalers ®

To my good friend William U. Rosemund (Chief of the US Army's Still Media Services Department) whose help throughout the years has allowed me to complete many a book on the US Army in action

First published in 1992 by Motorbooks International Publishers & Wholesalers, PO Box 2, 729 Prospect Avenue, Osceola, WI 54020 USA

© Michael Green, 1992

Motorbooks International books are also available at discounts in bulk quantity for industrial or sales-promotional use. For details write to Special Sales Manager at the Publisher's address

Library of Congress Cataloging-in-Publication Data
Green, Michael.
    Hummer / Michael Green.
      p.   cm.
    Includes index.
    ISBN 0-87938-592-8
    1. High Mobility Multipurpose Wheeled Vehicle. 2. United States—Armed Forces—Transportation—History—20th century. I. Title.
    UG618.G74   1992
    357'.54—dc20   91-48240

On the front cover: A Hummer M998 Cargo-Troop Carrier with a 30mm automatic cannon. *AM General*

On the back cover: The Hummer is designed to carry American soldiers over any terrain, from scorching desert to snowy mountains. *AM General and Greg Stewart*

Printed and bound in the United States of America

Contents

Acknowledgments

Special thanks for help in putting this book together are due to Craig C. MacNab, Suzanne Curry, Greg Stewart, Chuck Porter, Col. David Kiernan, Debbie De Loach, Casey Clugston, Jacques M. Littlefield and Ken Ditty.

Introduction

Operation Desert Storm was the first military conflict since World War II in which the US armed forces did not use their well-known jeeps. In service with American fighting forces since the earliest days of World War II, the venerable jeep and its various descendants are quickly disappearing from the US military inventory of wheeled vehicles. They are being replaced on today's battlefields by another vehicle whose name is slated to become a legend like that of the jeep.

Known by its military designation as the High Mobility Multipurpose Wheeled Vehicle (HMMWV), this vehicle is a lightweight, highly mobile, diesel-powered, four-wheel-drive tactical vehicle that uses a common one-and-a-quarter-ton payload chassis to carry a wide variety of military hardware ranging from machine guns to tube-launched, optically tracked, wire-guided (TOW) antitank guided missile launchers.

Since HMMWV is a mouthful to pronounce every time you want to talk about the vehicle, American soldiers quickly nicknamed the new vehicle the Humvee. The builders of the vehicle, AM General Corporation, refer to it as the HUMMER® (HUMMER® is a registered trademark of the AM General Corporation). The name Hummer does not stand for anything, but was merely chosen by the company to represent the product.

The first AM General built Hummer came off the assembly line—located in Mishawaka, near South Bend, Indiana—in 1984. When AM General got the contract to build the Hummer for the US military forces, it was the largest multiyear contract for tactical wheeled vehicles ever awarded by the US government, at 55,000 vehicles. AM General also had options for another 15,000 vehicles, picked up by the US military, bringing the total Hummer order to about 70,000 vehicles. In late 1989, AM General was awarded a new five-year contract that committed the US government to about 33,000 additional vehicles, raising the total contract order to over 100,000 Hummers.

The American military jeep in its final version was known as the M151A2. It is anticipated that the last 10,000 vehicles of this type will be phased out of the inventory by the end of 1994. Although most active-duty units in the US military establishment are now fully equipped with the Hummer, many National Guard and Reserve units will be forced to make do with the aging M151A2 jeep for a few more years.

The Hummer is a multiservice program that also provides vehicles to satisfy the US Marine Corps, US Navy and

US Air Force requirements. This follows in the footsteps of the jeep program, which also saw widespread use of its vehicles by all the various branches of the US armed forces from World War II days.

The basic version of the Hummer, which is the Cargo-Troop Carrier, can be sling-loaded by the UH-60 Black Hawk helicopter. All other versions of the Hummer can be sling-loaded by the US Army CH-47 Chinook medium-lift helicopter. All versions of the Hummer can be air-transported in the ubiquitous Lockheed C-130 Hercules transport plane (three can be carried) or the Air Force C-141 Starlifter plane (six can be carried) or C-5A Galaxy transport plane (fifteen can be carried).

The Hummer is a versatile vehicle whose chassis has spawned an entire line of different versions. Not all of these permutations have been accepted into service with the US armed forces. However, owing to the vehicle's sterling serv-

ice during Operation Desert Storm and its growing popularity among the soldiers who have become attached to it much like their fathers and grandfathers grew attached to their jeep, no doubt the Hummer will soon become a popular icon of American culture, as the jeep is.

In performance tests, the Hummer performance surpassed all other four-wheel-drive military vehicles. It is one of the most thoroughly tested vehicles to join the US military fleet.

Other countries that have bought Hummers are the Philippines (150), Mexico (more than 1,000), Thailand (150), Djibouti (ten), Luxembourg (twenty-nine) and Taiwan (more than 1,000).

Saudi Arabia is considering acquiring a large number of Hummers in various versions. Other countries in the Far East, Middle East, Latin America and Europe have also expressed interest in the Hummer.

Chapter 1

Hummer History

The Jeep

In 1940, with war clouds on the horizon, the US Army expressed interest in obtaining a small general-purpose vehicle. Three companies developed their concepts of such a vehicle. After testing all three models, the Army settled on the Willys-Overland quarter-ton four-wheel-drive design (plus features of other designs) and awarded Willys-Overland Motors (a distant ancestor of the AM General Corporation) a contract for 16,000, the first of a total quantity of 350,349 built during World War II. At the Army's request, Willys-Overland granted Ford Motor Company a license and the technical data necessary to provide a second source of sup-

World War II jeeps landing on Omaha Beach in France on June 12, 1944. US Army

ply, and Ford produced some 277,268 of the Willys-designed jeep during the war years.

The jeep quarter-ton truck was intended originally as a powerful reconnaissance car that also could replace the motorcycle of World War I. But its usefulness went far beyond that of reconnaissance or messenger carrier. It carried people and supplies. It carried the wounded. It mounted machine guns. It was a command car. It towed trailers. It served as a chaplain's altar in the field. It parked airplanes. And it performed a multitude of other duties, governed solely by the creative ingenuity of the military user. The vehicle was used by officers and statesmen of many allied nations, as well as by non-commissioned officers and enlisted people. Soldiers loved it!

This World War II jeep, with makeshift front fenders, is passing a burning German truck on the way to Worms, Germany, on March 20, 1945. US Army

One famous cartoon by Bill Mauldin showed a grieving Army sergeant standing with his back to his vehicle, one hand over his eyes and the other hand pointing a pistol at the hood of his beloved jeep. The jeep had suffered irreparable damage in combat, and the sergeant was about to put it out of its "misery" (much as he would a horse). The cartoon carried no caption. None was needed because Mauldin had captured on paper with a few strokes of his pen the true feeling of countless American soldiers for their rugged, go-anywhere vehicle.

Starting in 1945, Willys-Overland's postwar philosophy was shaped to relate the manufacture of its vehicle to peacetime needs at home and abroad, and to this end the company began development of the CJ (civilian jeep) vehicles. At

Soldiers of the Intelligence and Reconnaissance Platoon, 2nd Infantry Division, US Army display newly designed armored plates fitted to their jeeps. The date is January 1951, at the height of the Korean War. US Army

the same time, Willys-Overland introduced the industry's first steel-bodied station wagon. By 1950, Willys-Overland had reentered the civilian car market with its Aero-Willys line of passenger vehicles. The company was purchased in 1953 by Henry J. Kaiser and renamed Willys Motor Company.

The fifties led to more military programs in support of the Korean War and to the development of a new series of vehicles. For the duration of the Korean War and thereafter, the company continued its production of the M38 and M38A1 jeeps which were updated versions of the World War II military vehicle.

Although it closely resembled its World War II ancestors, the M38 featured a number of exterior body changes, plus a modified version of the World War II era four-cylinder, sixty-horsepower engine, which gave it a little

A World War II era Army jeep during a training session in the late fifties. Behind the jeep is an M59 armored personnel carrier.

Farther back, behind the M59, is an M48 Patton tank. US Army

An American-built M38 jeep in use by the Israeli Army during the 1967 Arab-Israeli War. Israeli Army

The civilian version of the M38 jeep. This vehicle was used as the official car of the Blue Angels Flight Demonstration Squadron in March of 1987. US Army

The M38 jeep was license-built in many countries around the world. Shown is a Japanese-built (Mitsubishi) version of the M38 jeep. Armed with a 106mm recoilless rifle and towing a trailer, this vehicle is being operated by soldiers from the Japanese Ground Self Defense Force. US Army

extra power. Shortly after the M38 was introduced, in 1952, the M38A1 jeep entered service. Featuring a four-cylinder, seventy-two-horsepower engine, the M38A1 also had a wider wheelbase than the M38. The M38A1 was built until 1958 and came in numerous models.

The Mule

For the average foot soldier, the US Army had long sought to provide a basic and simple vehicle to act as an equipment carrier. In the early fifties, Willys-Overland designed and built a prototype of a half-ton vehicle that eventually became known as the M274 Mechanical Mule. The M274 weighed about 750

Two examples of the M274 half-ton four-wheel-drive utility vehicle, nicknamed the Mule. These vehicles have just arrived in

South Vietnam in May 1965 and belong to the Army's 173rd Airborne Brigade. US Army

This Marine Corps M274 Mule is fitted with a 106mm recoilless rifle, which has just been fired at an enemy position in South Vietnam on May 1, 1967. USMC

pounds and could carry close to 1,000 pounds of cargo and personnel.

The Mule was primarily designed to be used by infantry and paratroop units where its light weight would allow it to be easily transported by planes or helicopters. It was also employed by the US Marine Corps. The Mule has been replaced in all branches of the US military by the Hummer. Altogether, almost 900 Mules saw service with the US military.

M151

The replacement for the M38A1 jeep was the Ford Motor Company de-

Marines patrol the streets of downtown Beirut, Lebanon, in 1983, in an M151 jeep. The Marines were deployed in Lebanon as part of a multinational peacekeeping force following confrontations between Israeli military and the Palestine Liberation Organization. USMC

signed M151 jeep. Most M151 jeeps were built by AM General. Originally meant to be called the Military Utility Tactical Truck (MUTT), the MUTT title never

Members of 2nd Platoon, 59th Military Police Company, pause with their M151 jeeps for a radio check at a marshaling area during exercise Reforger 1982. In the background stands Lt. Gen. N. R. Thompson, Jr., commander of the 21st Support Command Center. US Army

A Marine M151 jeep mounting a 40mm grenade launcher. USMC

stuck to the vehicle, and the soldiers continued to call it a jeep.

First produced in 1964, the M151 jeep—due to its higher performance, better ride and different handling characteristics when compared with its predecessor—unfortunately represented a serious challenge to soldier driving skills. In particular, the independent swingarm type rear suspension, although a performance improvement over the traditional solid axle type design, provided little driver feedback of vehicle dynamics and had a tendency for tire "tuck-under" when the vehicle was pushed to its limits.

Eventually, the American military corrected the tuck-under problem with the appearance of the M151A2 model, which entered production in 1969 and included a redesigned rear independent suspension system. This modification improved the M151's handling characteristics, but because of the vehicle's basic narrow width and high ground clearance for cross-country performance, vehicle stability under some conditions was still lacking. The M151A2s that remain in US National Guard and Reserve units have all been fitted with rollbar cages to protect their occupants.

The M151 series of jeeps saw widespread service with the American armed forces in many versions. But, the vehicle was still too small and light to fulfill all the military needs for cross-country transport of troops and equipment. As a result, the American military since the sixties fielded a number of vehicle types to satisfy its logistic needs.

Gama Goat

Another vehicle designed to keep up with the jeep on the battlefield was the

M561 Gama Goat. Placed into service by the US Army as a high-mobility, forward-area cargo carrier truck, the Gama Goat was a generalized copy of some foreign and commercial vehicle designs that focused on performance in the off-road environment.

The Gama Goat was built by the Consolidated Diesel Electric Company, Old Greenwich, Connecticut.

Because it was articulated in both roll and pitch, the M561 Gama Goat could cross all types of terrain without its wheels ever losing contact with the ground.

The M561 Gama Goat was built out of aluminum and could be made watertight for swimming and fording water barriers. In the water, it could be propelled by its spinning wheels at about two and a half miles per hour.

Although novel in concept, the M561 Gama Goat was not a success in service with either the US Army or Marine Corps. Not a very reliable vehicle, it was disliked by its crews because of the high noise levels produced by its engine, which was mounted at shoulder level immediately behind the driver's position.

The Hummer has replaced all the M561 Gama Goats in the US military inventory.

Militarized Civilian Trucks

In the late sixties and early seventies, the US Army decided to try fielding a fleet of commercially built four-wheel-drive trucks to fulfill various military requirements.

This was not the first time the US military had bought commercially made trucks. Specially designed vehicles like

The M561 Gama Goat is a six-wheel-drive, diesel-engine-driven, articulating joint cargo vehicle. Used by both the Army and the Marine Corps. US Army

the jeep, the Gama Goat, the Mechanical Mule and others are expensive to develop and build. This cost gets passed on to the US government, which is always looking for ways to reduce costs. Buying off-the-shelf civilian trucks has always seemed to offer some big cost savings. Unfortunately, the demands of military service take a heavy toll on modified civilian vehicles.

The first of the civilian four-wheel-drive trucks placed into military service was the M715. This was basically a Kaiser-built pickup truck modified to meet government specifications. First placed into service in 1967, it had a number of reliability problems, which caused it to be quickly phased out of service.

The M715 was replaced in 1975 by the modified civilian Dodge W200 series truck. Known by its military designation as the M880, this vehicle came in various versions including an ambulance variant. Almost 40,000 M880s saw US military service.

Eventually, the Dodge M880 series of vehicles was replaced by the Commercial Utility Cargo Vehicle (CUCV) and the Hummer. The CUCV is a one-and-a-quarter-ton (M1008 or M1028) or three-quarter-ton (M1009), all-wheel-drive, diesel-engine-driven vehicle. It is basically a commercial Chevy one-and-a-quarter-ton pickup truck or a Chevy three-quarter-ton Blazer with a military light and paint package. The diesel engine and other major components are the same as or similar to those in the Hummer. The CUCV can be transported inside a CH-47 or larger helicopter or a C-130 or larger aircraft but cannot be sling-loaded. It can travel at speeds of more than fifty-five miles per hour on improved roads and has limited off-road mobility.

The CUCV serves concurrently with the Hummer. It is used for general utility and command and control missions where specialized military vehicles, high off-road mobility or high cargo capacity are not required. The M1008 (a one-and-a-quarter-ton pickup truck) is used for general utility and troop transportation; the M1028 is identical to the M1008 except that it does not have a tailgate and is used to transport communications shelters; and the M1009 (a three-quarter-ton Blazer) is used for command and control and light utility operations.

The M715 four-wheel-drive Army pickup truck. US Army

The Army M880 was a modified civilian Dodge W200 pickup truck. Michael Green

Two versions of the commercial Utility Cargo Vehicle used by the Army. The vehicle in front is the M1009, basically a modified Chevrolet *Blazer. The vehicle behind it is the M1008 pickup truck.* Michael Green

The Beginning

Unhappy with the performance of the civilian trucks modified for military use and the M561 Gama Goat and concerned with the payload and size limitations of the M151 jeep and M274 Mule, the US Army decided in the late seventies that it needed a new jack-of-all-trades vehicle that could fulfill all the mission requirements of the civilian trucks and various specially designed Army vehicles. With this in mind, the US Army created a written requirement for an HMMWV that could serve a wide variety of military roles.

In 1980, three firms responded to the Army's requirements by submitting various vehicle proposals. The three firms were AM General, Chrysler Defense and Teledyne Continental.

The three firms submitted prototypes for the test and evaluation. These prototypes, although different in design approach particularly in engines and suspension, were responsive to the requirements.

The military was looking for a new diesel-engined family of versatile, technologically advanced cross-country vehicles capable of performing both combat and combat-support roles. The basic vehicle chassis was supposed to have the ability to be modified into a number of different variants.

The competition for the development of a vehicle meeting the demands of the Army's HMMWV performance specifications was great. Teledyne and Chrysler Defense (later sold to General Dynamics) already had designs in the developmental phase when AM General started.

The Teledyne prototype HMMWV was based on an earlier vehicle known as the Cheetah. Designed by Mobility Technology International of Santa Clara, California, in 1977, the Cheetah was bought by Teledyne who also involved the Lamborghini car company of Italy in its development.

Teledyne's HMMWV prototype was powered by an International Harvester Company 6.9 liter V-8 diesel engine, coupled to a General Motors 475 Turbo-Hydramatic three-speed automatic transmission. Its suspension system was independent all around with double A-arms and variable-rate torsion bars.

Teledyne prototype HMMWVs featured a steel frame with a lightweight aluminum body. It also had run-flat tires and an explosion-proof fuel tank.

General Dynamics's HMMWV prototype, taken over from Chrysler, was known as the XM998 and was powered by a North American Deutz F8L-610 air-cooled V-8 diesel engine coupled to a Chrysler A727 three-speed automatic transmission.

Front suspension on the General Dynamic XM998 was independent, with double A-arms, but at the rear a solid Dana 60 type axle (with a limited-slip differential) was combined with trailing arms and coil springs.

FMC's Dune Buggy

Although AM General, Teledyne Continental and General Dynamics (formerly Chrysler Defense) all had submitted proposed vehicle concepts to the Army, one company had really begun the development of a new all-terrain, multimission-capable vehicle to replace the jeep and other Army vehicles in various roles. This was FMC, which in 1970 presented a vehicle known as the XR311 Dune Buggy. FMC is best known for being the designer and builder of the M113 armored personnel carrier and the M2 and M3 Bradley Armored Fighting Vehicles.

Engineered and built by FMC using the best features of civilian-designed high-performance off-road wheeled vehicles, the XR311 had a very low silhouette (only sixty-three inches), a low center of gravity and power steering, plus a four-wheel independent suspension system. FMC also offered various special-purpose kits to adapt the XR311 to specific military roles, ranging from a scout vehicle kit to an antiarmor attack vehicle kit.

Unfortunately, owing to FMC's desire to concentrate on designing and building tracked vehicles, the XR311 was passed on to AM General, which in 1978 added some box-shaped armor protection to the vehicle and redesigned it as the XM966. The XR311 itself never went beyond the prototype stage, owing to lack of Army interest.

The First Hummer

The first prototype Hummer, an ancestor of the current configurations,

This early-model FMC prototype XR311 dune buggy is armed with a 106mm recoilless rifle. FMC

19

went for company testing at the Nevada Automotive Test Center (the largest private automotive test facility in the United States) in July of 1980, only eleven months from its inception, which for an all-new vehicle design was a feat.

The Army's procurement of test vehicles did not begin until February 1981, and the award for the most responsive designs was not made until June 1981. Development contracts were awarded to Chrysler Defense, Teledyne and, of course, AM General.

Eleven vehicles were acquired from each firm including TOW Missile Carriers, Cargo-Troop Carriers, and Mini and Maxi Ambulance Carrier variants. The requirements were comprehensive, with demands for light armor, vehicle weight constraints relying on material

application breakthroughs and even a solid-body ambulance that could be reduced in height for helicopter transport, not to mention the need for deep water fording ability, the need for Arctic and desert operational ability, and the most stringent reliability, durability and maintainability requirement ever placed upon a tactical military vehicle. All of this and ten months to do it in.

AM General was the first to complete its vehicles, in April 1982, and deliver them to the Army's proving grounds in Aberdeen, Maryland, Yuma, Arizona, and to the operational test site at Fort Hunter-Liggett, California.

The test phase, known as Development Testing and Operational Testing (DT/OT), took place over a five-month period, after which a call for production

AM General's version of the FMC XR311 was called the XM966. FMC

offerings was made from the competing contractors. The importance of completing the 20,000 mile testing on the durability vehicles was vital, as the Army would consider only the level of attainment during the prescribed test period. AM General was the first to complete the testing.

However, AM General was still faced with the most important hurdle: submitting a production proposal and winning the contract based upon a combination of the most technically qualified and most cost-effective five-year production offering. On March 22, 1983, AM General was awarded a $1.2 billion contract to produce about 55,000 Hummers over a five-year period, plus options on 15,000 more vehicles if so ordered.

The US General Accounting Office (GAO) decided in May 1983 to initiate a

An early prototype Hummer. AM General

review of the Hummer contract to determine whether results from the Hummer's development and operational tests justified placing the vehicle into production under a multiyear contract.

On April 23, 1984, the GAO issued a draft report that concluded that the Army's decision to award a full-scale production contract was premature, criticized AM General's Hummer design and reliability, and indicated that the lack of design stability did not justify use of a multiyear contract. The GAO failed to consider that AM General had made extensive changes to its Hummer design as a result of the experience gained during the DT/OT. Instead, the GAO focused its attention on the deficiencies found during the DT/OT, even though it was aware that these deficiencies had been corrected.

On May 10, 1984, the assistant secretary of the Army, in a memorandum for the under secretary of defense in charge of research and engineering, did not agree with the GAO allegations that the decision to produce the Hummer was premature:

The production decision was based on a review of test results as well as analysis of proposed corrections to DT/OT testing deficiencies. The Hummer accelerated acquisition process, the production decision, and the follow-on testing represent a prudent, carefully conceived approach that was designed to field a supportable and mission capable vehicle in a cost-effective manner. We are confident that our objectives have been realized in the Hummer.

On June 14, 1984, Senator William V. Roth asked the US Senate to prohibit obligation of funds for production of the Hummer until reliability was proven in additional tests.

On June 21, 1984, the US Senate rejected by a vote of fifty-one to thirty-eight Senator Roth's amendment, which would have delayed funds for production of the Hummer.

AM General shipped twelve Hummers (seven utility vehicles and five weapon carriers) to the Aberdeen and Yuma proving grounds in July 1984 for Initial Production Testing (IPT) scheduled to last approximately six months.

At an early date during the tests, a driveshaft broke on a Hummer undergoing durability testing at Aberdeen while reportedly being driven in excess of seventy miles per hour. Further Hummer testing was temporarily halted by the Army pending analysis of the cause of the driveshaft failure.

At the request of the Army, AM General engineers attempted to duplicate the Aberdeen test conditions at the privately owned Nevada Test Center and to induce failure by operating five Hummers at speeds of from seventy-seven to eighty miles per hour. During the tests, three of the five Hummers broke their driveshaft.

Although no driveshaft ever broke while the vehicle was being driven at design-specified maximum speeds and the contractor had no legal requirement to modify the design, the Army and AM General Division quickly began replacing driveshafts on all the test Hummers at Aberdeen in anticipation of resuming testing.

The Army resumed testing at Aberdeen, limiting speeds to the contract specifications of sixty-five miles per hour.

The Hummer was officially introduced internationally by Senator Barry Goldwater at a ceremony at the 1984 Farnborough Air Show outside of London. Later, Senator Goldwater drove the Hummer over a test course at a nearby British military test center. About twenty American and foreign journalists also test-drove the Hummer at the same course during the week-long air show.

On September 6, 1984, five Hummers arrived at Fort Hunter-Liggett for the Follow-on Test and Evaluation phase. Fort Hunter-Liggett is run by the US Army Test and Experimentation Command. At the base, a combined military-scientific team has the mission of providing hard, factual answers to the Army leadership on the performance of various items of equipment being considered for service.

To test the Hummers assigned to Fort Hunter-Liggett, each of the five vehicles was driven 6,000 miles cross-country during a six-week period. After these tests were completed, two Hummers were sent to the Army's Yuma Proving Grounds for durability testing.

Over 40,000 miles were logged on the two Hummers involved in this phase.

Since the Marine Corps would also be using the Hummer, two vehicles were sent to Camp Pendleton, California, and the Naval Amphibious Base located at Coronado, California, where the military conducted 1,200 miles of beach mobility testing.

In late 1984, three Hummers accumulated 3,000 miles of mobility testing at Fort Knox, Kentucky, over European-type terrain while another four Hummers completed a total of 80,792 miles of tests at the Army's Aberdeen Proving Grounds.

As a result of all the testing, the critics were silenced by the Hummer's outstanding reliability and strength throughout the tests.

In 1990, President George Bush ate his Thanksgiving Day turkey from the hood of a Hummer while visiting American troops in Saudi Arabia. Bob Hope, who traveled around Saudi Arabia entertaining American soldiers in various Hummers, referred to the vehicle as his "armored golf cart."

Chapter 2

Hummer Description

The macho-looking Hummer would never win any contests for beauty. Certainly nobody would ever call it cute.

The engine compartment of a Hummer. The Hummer is powered by a General Motors 379 cubic inch (6.2 liter) V-8 diesel that produces 150 horsepower. Michael Green

During Operation Desert Storm American soldiers called it Son of Jeep or a jeep on steroids. But this squat, brutal-looking vehicle was designed for the world's toughest environment: WAR.

Many well-known cross-country races demand a lot from both vehicles and drivers. Many civilian-built four-wheel-drive vehicles perform well during these contests. But, at the end of the race, the driver gets to go home to a cold beer and a warm bed, and the vehicle itself returns to some garage for maintenance.

Not so the Hummer. This mechanically superior vehicle must perform in a wide variety of terrain, from desert waste to jungle, for long periods of time with a minimum of maintenance. Not only does it have to carry its cargo and occupants in safety across difficult ground, but it also has to be able to dodge bullets and bombs. Whereas many four-wheel-drive vehicles have to worry about getting a flat tire from a nail or other sharp objects, the Hummer on a battlefield has to worry about running over a land mine.

Engine

The Hummer is powered by a General Motors 379 cubic inch (6.2 liter), 150 horsepower, liquid-cooled diesel V-8 engine with cast iron block and heads. The same proven engine is used in the US military CUCV family of civilian modified trucks. Many commercially sold trucks and vans are also equipped with this same engine. With a peak torque value of 265 pounds feet at 2000 rpm, the Hummer has incredible rough terrain climbing ability. Geared hubs also provide an effective torque multiplication of 1.92.1 at the ground.

The Hummer engine is coupled to a General Motors three-speed THM400 automatic transmission, ducting power to four drive wheels through a New Process 218 two-speed transfer case. The Hummer has one reverse gear.

An Army Hummer crossing a floating bridge in South Korea during Team Spirit 1988. Hummers have a maximum speed of sixty-five miles per hour on level ground and can travel about 300 miles on a twenty-five-gallon fuel tank. US Army

An Army military police Hummer of the 2nd Armored Division in West Germany during exercise Certain Strike, held in September 1987. The average Hummer weighs in at about 5,200 pounds and can carry a top payload of 2,500 pounds. US Army

A heavily laden Army Hummer prepares to take its place in the ground attack stage of Operation Desert Storm. During the conflict in the Middle East, Hummers were constantly overloaded by their crews. Yet the strong design of the Hummers allowed them to continue their missions. US Army

A 9th Infantry Division Hummer crossing a stream near Ipo, South Korea, during the 1986 Team Spirit exercises. On uneven terrain the *Hummer can reach speeds up to thirty miles per hour.* US Army

A TOW-equipped Army Hummer at speed. TOW antitank missiles fired from Hummers during the ground war phase of Operation *Desert Storm accounted for a number of Iraqi armored vehicles.* US Army

With the V-8 engine, the Hummer can reach speeds of over sixty-five miles per hour on paved roads. It can accelerate from zero to thirty miles per hour in seven seconds on a level surface. On uneven ground, it can attain a speed of thirty miles per hour depending on the terrain.

The Hummer is fitted with a plastic twenty-five-gallon fuel tank that gives the vehicle a range of about three hundred miles.

Because of its name, some people may think that the military Hummer hums! In reality, when driving a Hummer cross-country, the noise level is deafening. There is no sound deadening material anywhere in the Hummer. As a result, you can hear the engine and transmission, all the various vehicle components rattling and every rock or other obstruction you drive over. During cold weather conditions, when the windows on your Hummer are up and the heater is on, all these various sounds are even louder. In field operations, the radios normally found in most Hummers constantly squawk out instructions and orders. Combined with the noise of other military ground vehicles, like tanks or helicopters flying overhead, the Hummer is not a place for quiet contemplation but more like a mobile heavy metal music concert.

All the basic unarmed Hummers, except the hard-top ambulance variant, use metal-framed fabric doors with plastic windows that zip open and closed. Michael Green

This unarmed Army Hummer, equipped with fabric doors, is being used to tow a mobile field generator. Michael Green

A hard-top Hummer ambulance. The Hummer ambulance is fitted with a basic armor package, and has aluminum doors. Michael Green

A mobile fire team composed of Air Force base-security troops exit their Hummer at Sembach Air Force Base in West Germany in September 1988 during a training session.

Because of the large stamped X on the door, you can tell that this vehicle is an Armament Carrier with only the basic armor protection kit. USAF

Packed side by side are two early prototype Hummers. The one on the right is the Armament Carrier, the other is an unarmed Cargo-Troop Carrier version. Hummer prototypes

can normally be identified by having four holes in the front bumper. Production models have only three holes in the bumper. AM General

Even at idle, the military Hummer has a higher decibel level than any civilian vehicle now on the market.

Suspension

The Hummer has an independent suspension system, front and rear, with double A-arms, coil springs and hydraulic double-acting shock absorbers also fitted both front and rear.

The suspended carrier front and rear driveshafts are identical and interchangeable parts, connected to differentials that are mounted high directly in the chassis frame, increasing ground clearance and preventing damage to both shaft and differential. Hummer handling is enhanced by the front stabilizer bar that is attached to the lower control arms and pivot bracket, reducing shock from the lower A-frame member of the chassis.

Because of the Hummer's outstanding mobility over all types of terrain, both in field training and combat, Hummers used in the scouting role have

An Army Hummer Armament Carrier has just arrived in Belgium during a NATO exercise. Hummers are about six feet high, fifteen feet long and seven feet wide. US Army

proved quite successful. Used to reconnoiter enemy positions, Hummers have been able to go places that no other wheeled or tracked vehicle in US or foreign military service could go. Hummers serve in the scout units of both US Army armor and mechanized infantry divisions.

The Hummer uses a twenty-four-volt electrical system. It also has power hydraulic disc brakes on both front and rear wheels. The steering is of the recirculating ball power assisted type.

Wheels

The Hummer is normally fitted with four thirty-six-inch-tall, twelve-and-a-half-inch-wide Goodyear Wrangler RT II all-terrain bias tires, mounted on sixteen-and-a-half-inch rims. The tires are of the run-flat type, enabling the Hummer to be run with flat tires up to thirty miles at speeds of thirty miles per hour. No spare tire is carried in the Hummer. The Hummer can also be fitted with steel-belted radial tires.

During Operation Desert Storm, at least one US Army Hummer that ran over an Iraqi mine was able to be driven back miles by its wounded crew to a first aid station despite extensive damage to both the vehicle's front tires and suspension system.

Newer models of the Hummer entering service with the US military may be fitted with the AM General developed and patented Central Tire Inflation System (CTIS). With this, the vehicle operator can control tire pressure from inside the Hummer cab while the vehicle is on the move. Lowered tire pressure improves mobility in adverse conditions such as sand, mud and snow. It also

Looking into a Hummer from the passenger's side. The Hummer's drivetrain is in a midship position, allowing the vehicle's front differential to be raised. This, together with geared hubs, provides a sixteen-inch ground clearance. Michael Green

A US Army Hummer cab without a radio mount. The location of the Hummer crew on each side of the drivetrain allows the vehicle a very low center of gravity. Michael Green

A Marine Armament Carrier, mounting an M2 .50cal machine gun. This photo shows both the supplemental armor kit (the flat steel plates on the door) and the deep water fording kit. USMC

This Marine Armament Carrier in Saudi Arabia mounts an M2 .50cal machine gun with a night-vision scope attached to it. The vehicle has both the supplementary armor kit and the deep water fording kit, which are permanently fixed on all Marine Hummers. USMC

A Hummer Cargo-Troop Carrier with the four-person soft-top cab. USMC

The Hummer Cargo-Troop Carrier is used by the Army to tow the M167 20mm Vulcan antiaircraft gun. The weapon system is *mounted on a two-wheel carriage. When deployed, it is stabilized by three jacks.* Michael Green

greatly reduces the effects of road shock and vibration on the crew, vehicle and cargo when traveling over rough terrain.

Chassis

The Hummer is six feet tall (ambulance Hummers are taller), fifteen feet long and seven feet wide. This wide stance provides a very stable, road hugging vehicle that is almost impossible to roll over.

In contrast, the old M151 jeep was five feet, nine inches tall, eleven feet, 11/16 inches long and four feet, four inches

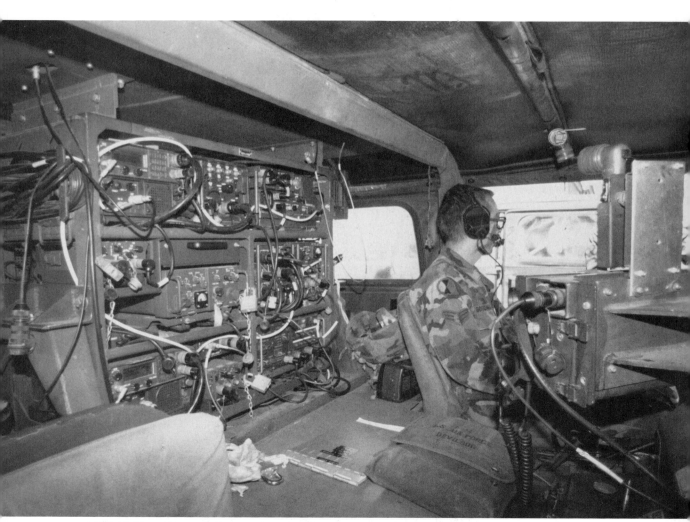

A US Air Force Hummer Cargo-Troop Carrier with a soft-top enclosure being used as a mobile ground-to-air communications vehicle. Michael Green

The AM General manufacturing facility located in Mishawaka, Indiana, with a string of *Hummers coming down the production line.* AM General

wide. While this small size made the M151 jeep very nimble in confined spaces, it also made the vehicle somewhat unstable and prone to roll over.

The M151 jeep under ideal conditions could carry 800 pounds of payload and tow in a small trailer another 1,000 pounds. The Hummer, which weighs about 5,200 pounds, can carry a payload of 2,500 pounds of personnel, weapons and cargo.

The Hummer is constructed on a steel frame. The body shell is composed of aluminum with a fiberglass hood. The

These AM General employees are making their final visual inspections on completed Hummers at the factory. AM General

Hummer is fastened together with rivets and industrial glue.

AM General builds the Hummer at its modern assembly plant in Mishawaka, Indiana, which is dedicated exclusively to the production of the vehicles. The facility includes state-of-the-art manufacturing equipment that makes extensive use of robotics and computerization.

A string of Chevy 6.2 liter V-8 diesel engines ready to be placed into Hummers on the production line. AM General

At AM General's manufacturing facility in Mishawaka, state-of-the-art manufacturing processes, including robotic welding and camouflage painting, are used. AM General

Chapter 3

In-Service Hummers

The Hummer in US military service is configured through the use of a common chassis with common components and different add-on kits to become six different vehicle types: the Cargo-Troop Carrier, the Armament Carrier, the TOW Missile Carrier, the Ambulance Carrier, the Shelter Carrier and the newest version to enter service, the Heavy Hummer Variant.

Based upon these six types, more than twenty subtypes have been developed, many of which differ from one another only in minor details. For example, seven different subtypes of the Cargo-Troop Carrier and eight different

The most numerous Hummer variant in US military service is the M998 Cargo-Troop Carrier. The M998 comes in a number of different forms. Depending on its mission, a number of fabric tops can be fitted to cover either soldiers or cargo. Michael Green

subtypes of the Armament Carrier are available.

Besides these standard model differences, specially modified Hummers serve as platforms for Army weapon systems or act even as stand-ins for enemy wheeled vehicles during Army training exercises.

Cargo-Troop Carrier

The most numerous Hummer variant in US military service is the M988 Cargo-Troop Carrier. Fitted with a winch, the same vehicle is known as the M1038. Considered the workhorse of the Hummer family, the M988 and M1038 can be configured in a number of ways.

All Hummers have the provision for having four doors. For some variants of the Hummer where the two rear doors are not needed, aluminum or simple wood fillets are used to close off these doors.

Depending on its mission and weather conditions, the M988 and M1038 Hummers can be open- or close-topped and fitted with a removable roll bar. The front windshield can also be folded down if needed. In simulated war games conducted at the National Training Center at Fort Irwin, California, the reflection from Hummer windshields could be seen for over eight miles distance at sunrise and sunset, a deadly giveaway for any

This Army Hummer Cargo-Troop Carrier is carrying the frame for a military communications shelter. The Army is heavily dependent on command and control equipment. It is just as important as ammunition and fuel on the modern battlefield. Michael Green

This Army Hummer has a soft-top enclosure over the rear of the vehicle to protect its cargo or occupants from the elements. The battery compartment is located under the right front passenger's section. Michael Green

This Army Hummer is being used as a troop carrier and has just been air-dropped into a landing field. US Navy

These Cargo-Troop Carriers are being driven into the rear of a US Air Force C-5A Galaxy.

Fifteen Hummers can be carried aboard a C-5A transport. US Army

A Cargo-Troop Carrier mounting a winch. The Hummer can travel up a sixty-percent

grade or travel along a forty-percent side grade. Michael Green

enemy observer looking for US military positions. As standard practice, all US military Hummers in the field must raise their front hood when parked for any length of time. The raising of the vehicle's hood is designed to cut down on reflection.

The M988 and M1038 are normally fitted with a number of different fabric tops. The tops come in high- or low-profile versions and are supported by metal lateral bows.

As a troop carrier, the M988 and M1038 can carry a two-person crew and eight seated passengers on wooden bench seats. As a cargo and troop carrier, the M988 and M1038 can be fitted with a four-seater fabric top and the small cargo space in the rear of the vehicle can be either covered or uncovered.

The M988 and M1038 can also be fitted with a weapon-station mount for machine guns.

Armament Carrier

The second most common Hummer variant is the M1025 Armament Carrier. With a winch it is known as the M1026. The Armament Carrier is configured for transportation of appropriate weapons with their supporting crews and equipment. The armament mounting kit features a thirty-two-inch

A Marine operates an M2 .50cal machine gun mounted on an Armament Carrier at Camp Pendleton, during a training exercise. The armament mounting kit fitted to all

Hummer armament carriers features a thirty-two-inch weapon ring with pintle mount and quick release cradle. Mounted weapons have a 360 degree arc of fire. USMC

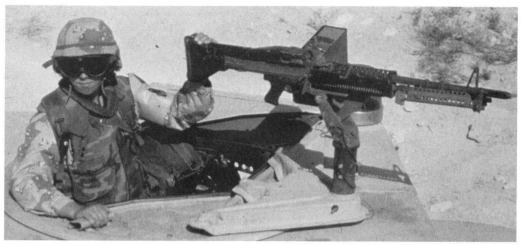

This Army military policewoman in Saudi Arabia is positioned in a Hummer Armament Carrier equipped with an M60 7.62mm machine gun. US Army

This 40mm automatic grenade launcher is being crewed by a military policeman during a training session. Michael Green

weapon ring with a pintle mount and a quick-release cradle. Mounted weapons have a 360 degree arc of fire. The mounting kit can accommodate one at a time the 40mm automatic grenade launcher, the M2 .50cal machine gun, the M60 7.62mm machine gun and the M240 7.62mm machine gun. Some US Army Cavalry units have also begun to experiment with carrying light motorcycles on the rear of their vehicles.

TOW Missile Carrier

The M966 TOW Missile Carrier was designed as a combat vehicle for the transportation of Army and Marine Corps antitank missile teams. With a winch, the vehicle is known as the M1036.

The TOW missile has been the main antitank weapon used by the US Army since the early seventies. Work first began on the missile in 1965, and it reached the production stage at the tail end of the Vietnam War. A few TOW missiles were rushed to South Vietnam in 1970, where they were quickly fitted to US Army Cobra gunships and took a heavy toll of attacking North Vietnamese tanks.

A military policeman operates a 40mm grenade launcher atop his Armament Carrier while on a training patrol at Fort Ord. This weapon is officially called the Mark 19 Model 3 40mm Heavy Machine Gun. It can fire six high-explosive grenades per second. Michael Green

Marines in Thailand in September 1989, during a joint Thai and US training operation. This Armament Carrier is armed with a 40mm grenade launcher. US Navy

A UH-60 Army Black Hawk helicopter lifts a Hummer of the 7th Infantry Division during a training exercise. US Army

Air Force loaders back a Marine Armament Carrier up the rear cargo ramp of a C-141B Starlifter aircraft during a joint Air Force and Marine Corps exercise. USAF

A CH-53E Super Stallion helicopter lowers a Marine Armament Carrier to the ground, during the amphibious assault exercise Operation Kernel Blitz 1987. USMC

Besides being mounted on attack helicopters and armed Hummers, the TOW is also fitted to tracked vehicles like the M113 and the M2 and M3 Bradley Armored Fighting Vehicles.

With a range of almost 5,000 yards on newer models, the TOW missile carries a high-explosive, armor-piercing, shaped-charge warhead that when it hits an enemy tank, produces a concentrated heat stream that can burn through all but the latest composite armor.

Weighing a little over forty-five pounds, the TOW missile is fired from a fiberglass launch tube. Attached to the launcher unit is a high-powered optical sight and sensor that allows a TOW gunner to keep the cross hairs on an enemy target. A computer in the launcher unit corrects any deviation of the missile in flight from the cross hair aim point and sends corrections to the missile by means of two extremely thin wires that deploy in flight.

The TOW missile is powered by two rocket motors, one of which burns out by the time it has left the launcher unit. The second motor does not start until it has traveled a certain distance away from the launch point. This protects the TOW gunner by making it difficult for enemy

Used by both the Army and the Marine Corps, the TOW Missile Carrier can carry six reload missiles. Greg Stewart

Members of the Army 10th Mountain Division, prepare a TOW antitank missile launcher mounted atop a Hummer Armament Carrier. US Army

A TOW launcher on its ground mount. The TOW launcher and guidance system weighs in at about 160 pounds. From its ground mount the TOW uses a four-person crew. Michael Green

observers to trace a visible smoke trail back to its point of origin.

The TOW can be fired from the Hummer on a ground tripod and is crewed by four people. With a combined weight of under 200 pounds for the missile and launcher unit, the TOW system can be quickly disassembled and moved to different locations.

The Hummer TOW Missile Carrier carries the entire TOW crew with the complete weapon system and associated equipment. Stowage in the cargo compartment of the vehicle is designed to facilitate the rapid TOW mounting and reloading. All TOW carriers have a two-way cargo door for up-loading the missiles and reloading the TOW launcher itself. The TOW crew can rapidly dismount the system for ground use, if needed. There are provisions for carrying six reload missiles in the M966 TOW missile carrier Hummer.

According to confirmed reports, TOW-equipped Hummers destroyed a number of Iraqi tanks during Operation Desert Storm.

Armored Hummers

All the basic unarmed Hummers, except the hard-top ambulance variant, use metal-framed soft fabric doors, with plastic windows that zip open and closed.

The aluminum and fiberglass doors on the hard-top ambulances, and on the various armed variants, bear a distinctive X-shaped stamping to increase the rigidity. The aluminum and fiberglass

An Armament Carrier fitted with a TOW missile launcher. The crew have removed both the front doors and the front windshield for better visibility in the desert landscape of Fort Irwin. Greg Stewart

A Marine operates a TOW missile launcher atop an Armament Carrier during Operation Cold Winter 1987. USMC

components on the Hummer provide a certain degree of armor protection from fragments, but are not bullet-proof like an M1 tank would be.

The aluminum and fiberglass doors on armed Hummer variants have a polycarbonate bullet-resistant window that slides up and down on metal tracks. The front windshield is also bullet resistant.

The US Marine Corps armed Hummer variants have been equipped with an additional supplemental armor kit consisting of thin, flat steel plates affixed to the doors and other surfaces. This armor kit provides a degree of protection from fragments, but not from bullets.

The flat steel plates and special deep water fording kits often fitted to US Marine Corps Hummers are the best way to distinguish them from the US Army Hummers.

The deep water fording kit consists of an exhaust pipe extension that runs all the way to the top of the rear of the vehicle on the driver's side. On the passenger's side is an extended air intake pipe located at the rear of the engine hood. With the deep water fording kit, the Hummer can cross sixty inches of water. Without it the Hummer can cross thirty inches of water.

Both Army and Marine Corps armed Hummer variants have a hood grille with louvers that are backed up by

Two brand-new Ambulance Carriers. The ambulance on the left is a Maxi variant that is going to be delivered to the Marine Corps.

The ambulance on the right is a Mini variant. AM General

baffles to prevent bullets or shell fragments from damaging the vehicle's radiator.

Ambulance Carrier

The Hummer ambulance family includes three variants: the M1035 Soft-Top, M996 Mini and M997 Maxi Ambulances. Each ambulance variant offers the outstanding off-road capability Hummer is known for.

The Soft-Top Ambulance is a basic Hummer fitted with a low-profile soft-top enclosure equipped to carry two litter patients, three ambulatory patients and a driver. It transports patients quickly from field to hospital. Only the Marine Corps uses this variant.

The Mini and Maxi Ambulances mount special shelters on the Hummer platform and are equipped to provide more comprehensive medical care. The Mini Ambulance is a low-profile, battlefront ambulance that can be deployed using the Low Altitude Parachute Extraction System (LAPES) or by means of a conventional airdrop, depending on the need.

Special storage areas and compartments are provided on both Mini and Maxi Ambulances, along with a heavy-duty suspension system, a 200 amp alternator and fragmentation protection. An integral environment control unit in the Maxi Ambulance provides air conditioning and heating for comfortable mobile conditions.

Shelter Carrier

The M1037 Shelter Carrier is equipped with a heavy-duty suspension system, a heavy-duty airlift bumper and built-in brackets to secure the shelter to

The driver's seat on an Army Ambulance Carrier. Michael Green

Inside an Army Mini Ambulance Carrier. Michael Green

An Army Mini Ambulance Carrier under the cover of a camouflage net at Fort Ord during a field training session. Michael Green

The M1035 soft-top version of the Hummer ambulance. The soft-top ambulance is in reality a slightly converted M998 Cargo-Troop Carrier. AM General

This Army Hummer Mini Ambulance Carrier has been converted to a command and communication vehicle by the 7th Infantry Division (Light). Greg Stewart

This Shelter Carrier is taking part in desert training at Fort Irwin. Greg Stewart

Another Shelter Carrier at Fort Irwin, California. The crew's personal gear is strapped to *the top of the shelter. The vehicle is towing a mobile field generator.* Greg Stewart

This Shelter Carrier is outfitted as a mobile switchboard system. The vehicle is hidden under a camouflage net. Michael Green

the Hummer chassis. With a winch the vehicle is known as the M1042. The shelter carrier mounted on the mobile Hummer vehicle normally carries communication gear such as radios, battlefield computers and a variety of other electronic equipment that requires greater protection from the elements than would be provided by a simple plastic top as fitted to the M988 and M1038 Hummer Cargo-Troop Carrier. The shelter is secured to the Hummer by cables with turnbuckles and can be removed if necessary.

Heavy Hummer

Because of increasing weight-carrying demands, AM General has modified its existing Hummer chassis to increase the gross vehicle weight to 10,000 pounds, thus resulting in the M1097

The interior of the Shelter Carrier outfitted with a switchboard system. Michael Green

The Heavy Hummer Variant. Outwardly, a standard Hummer and the Heavy variant look the same. Michael Green

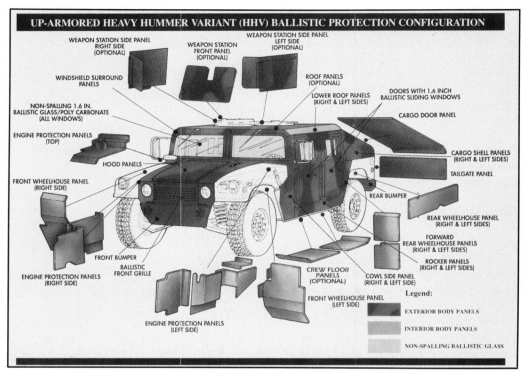

An AM General diagram showing the armor in the up-armored Heavy Hummer. AM General

Heavy Hummer Variant. This was accomplished with minimum changes to the chassis. The Heavy Hummer retains the standard 150 horsepower diesel engine.

The Heavy Hummer can accommodate a larger number of communication shelters, weapon systems and logistics support systems and boasts increased ballistic protection and towing capabilities.

One of the newest shelters fitted to the HHV and Shelter Carrier is the Army's Standardized Integrated Command Post System (SICPS) shelter. The SICPS is a family of command-post facilities developed to house the Army Tactical Command and Control System. The shelter is equipped with a five-kilowatt power unit, an air-conditioner unit, a collective chemical-biological protection system, equipment racks, and power and signal import-export panels, plus intercom and operator seats.

AM General has taken advantage of its Heavy Hummer chassis to develop an armor protection system for its weapon carriers. This system consists of ballistic panels that are applied to the various

HHV armament and TOW Missile Carriers to defeat both 7.62mm and 5.56mm ball ammo.

The additional ballistic materials are selectively applied to both the exterior and the interior of the vehicle. Maximum protection from ground attack is provided to the crew and vital automotive components. Optimum visibility and protection are provided by windshield and side windows made of 1.6 inch non-spalling ballistic glazing material. Roof, crew floor and weapon station armor protect against weapons as powerful as the 7.62mm.

The up-armored Heavy Hummer has successfully completed AM General's full-scale live-firing tests and independent durability and performance testing. A small number of Heavy Hummers have already been sold to an unnamed foreign country. As of yet, the US military has not purchased any up-armored HHV.

Prime Mover

The Hummer is the designated prime mover for the US Army's 105mm light artillery howitzers. It provides Army and Marine Corps field artillery

The limited production Hummer Prime Mover is used to tow the Army's light howitzers. Michael Green

This Prime Mover belongs to the 7th Infantry Division and has been deployed for training to NTC. Greg Stewart

The main identifying feature of the Prime Mover is the stowage rack located over the cab of the vehicle. Other Hummers do not have this rack. Greg Stewart

The M119 is a towed 105mm howitzer that is based on the British L119. Michael Green

This Army Hummer Prime Mover is being used to tow a supply trailer. Greg Stewart

units with the ability to move these weapons over all but the roughest terrain.

The US Army is mainly using the standard M998 Cargo-Troop Carrier. During Operation Desert Shield and Operation Desert Storm, other versions of the Hummer were used to tow 105mm light artillery howitzers.

With the introduction of the new M119 Light Artillery Howitzers, the US Army tested a specially designed Hummer known as the M1069. This variant failed in field-testing with the Army's 7th Infantry Division (Light) and 82nd Airborne Division because of crew complaints about the harsh ride characteristics when towing the howitzer. The Army has decided that a version of the

new Heavy Hummer will tow the M119 howitzer in the future.

The M119 is an American-made copy of the British-built L119 Light Gun. It is a lightweight, 105mm, towed howitzer that improves fire support for the Army's airborne, air assault and light infantry divisions and separate brigades. It will replace all older generation M102 howitzers in the active force. It can fire all conventional 105mm ammunition currently in the Army inventory and the new high-explosive rocket-assisted ammunition now in production.

Because of its light weight and low profile, the Heavy Hummer and M119 will be transportable in the C-130 and the C-141B aircraft and by the CH-47

Before the arrival of the M119, the Hummer was used to tow the American-designed M102 105mm howitzer. This Prime Mover is towing an M102 to a live-fire range in Panama in May 1989. USAF

and CH-53 helicopters. A lot fewer missions will be required to lift a battalion of Hummers and M119 howitzers than to deploy the same size unit equipped with larger prime movers.

Smoke Carrier

The Hummer Shelter Carrier is also employed by the US Army fitted with smoke generators.

Smoke has a variety of uses on the modern battlefield. In the attack, it can conceal vehicles, deceiving the enemy about the strength and location of friendly forces. It is also used to blind enemy observers and spoil their aim. In the defense, it can confuse, slow and blind attacking elements and conceal defensive positions and movements.

Smoke's effectiveness depends on the weather. Wind direction and speed are important considerations. If the wind is strong or from the wrong direction, it may be impossible to establish an effective smoke screen. The best time to use smoke is when the ground is cooler than the air. Warmer air holds the smoke close to the ground.

Soviet-Style Variant

The strangest Hummer variants in service with the US Army are located at Fort Irwin in southern California, home of the National Training Center (NTC). Here, in an area of almost 1,000 square

The Shelter Carrier is also employed by the Army with smoke generators. This Hummer is laying down a smoke screen during a training exercise at NTC. US Army

A number of unarmed Hummers have been modified at NTC to represent Soviet BRDM-2 scout cars during training exercises. Michael Green

A real Soviet-built BRDM-2 scout car on display at NTC. Michael Green

miles of sun-baked terrain, the Army constructed the world's most sophisticated and realistic simulated battlefield.

To provide worthy, realistic opposition for the troops coming to the NTC for training, the Army created a unit designated as the Opposing Force (OPFOR). The members of the OPFOR represent major elements of a Soviet Army motorized regiment. Since it is not practical to use large quantities of real Soviet-built equipment in training, the Army modified a number of American vehicles into vague copies of their Soviet Army counterparts.

Since the Soviet Army has always employed a large number of wheeled scout cars, the US Army uses a small number of Hummer M998 Cargo-Troop Carriers fitted with fiberglass bodywork to replicate or simulate Soviet BRDM-2 scout cars. The modified Hummers employed by the OPFOR at the NTC have accurately portrayed their Soviet counterparts in hundreds of NTC training exercises.

Stinger Missile Carrier

The Stinger antiaircraft missile as used by the US Army is a shoulder-launched system. The two-person Stinger teams use an M998 Cargo-Troop Carrier for transport. Each of these vehicles is equipped with two radios and a basic missile load of eight Stingers carried in four-round racks that fit in the rear cargo bay of the Hummer.

The Stinger is a shoulder-fired, infrared missile antiaircraft system. The missile homes on the heat emitted by

A modified Hummer serves as a Soviet Army BRDM-2 scout car at Fort Lewis, Washington, during a combat training exercise. US Army

The Hummer can carry eight additional Stinger missile reloads in its rear cargo bay. Michael Green

An Army Hummer used to carry a Stinger missile crew and reload missiles. The Stinger launcher units are carried in the side storage boxes, with additional missiles carried in the rear of the cargo bay. Michael Green

either jet- or propeller-driven aircraft and helicopters. A Stinger crew visually acquires its target and electronically interrogates it to help determine if it is a friend. The missile notifies the gunner when it has a "lock" on the target. After the trigger is pulled, the Stinger is ejected from the tube by a small launch motor. Once the missile has traveled a safe distance from the gunner, its main engine ignites and propels it to the target. The Stinger is stored in a sealed tube, requires no maintenance in the field and is designed to withstand the rigors of the battlefield.

The Avenger

One new Hummer variant in service with the US Army is the Avenger antiaircraft system. The Avenger sys-

An Avenger air defense system deployed with Battery A, 2nd Battalion, of the 6th Air Defense Artillery in Saudi Arabia. The Avenger consists of a four-tube Stinger anti-aircraft missile launcher mounted on each side of an operator's station on a pedestal carried by a Hummer. An M2 .50cal machine gun can be mounted beneath the right side Stinger launcher. US Army

A Hummer of the US Army's 24th Division in Saudi Arabia, mounting an Avenger anti-aircraft system. US Army

tem consists of eight ready-to-fire Stinger missiles and a .50 caliber machine gun integrated with sensors and target acquisition devices.

The integrated Avenger system provides all the necessary functions to detect, acquire, track and identify friend or foe aircraft with either the missile or the machine gun during the day or night and in adverse weather. Its standard vehicle-mounted launchers interface and can function with all the various models of the Stinger.

The Avenger system, which is mounted on the Hummer M1037 Shelter Carrier, has a two-person crew that can fire its missiles on the move or operate the missile system from a distance with a remote control device. The Avenger system is built by Boeing Aerospace Company and went into full-scale production in April 1990.

Chapter 4

Hummer Prototypes

AM General has designed a number of other special kits to extend the mission capability and flexibility of the Hummers. Many of these are entering service or are under consideration by the military.

Two special kits entering into US Army service are add-on brushguards

An up-armored Heavy Hummer prototype undergoing field-testing by AM General. AM General

and add-on underbody skid protection consisting of high-strength tubular steel guards for the Hummer engine, transmission and axles, plus metal guards for the fuel tank and transfer case.

Other Hummer kits not yet accepted into military service are spare tire and jerry can carriers that can be fitted to the rear of a Hummer with special bumpers.

At different times, AM General has also proposed the mounting of a 25mm or 30mm cannon or 7.62mm Gatling gun on the Hummer.

Crossbow

Another air defense system proposed for use by the US Army is the LTV Crossbow pedestal-mounted weapon system mounted on a Hummer chassis. The Crossbow system was designed as a lightweight pedestal-mounted platform and drive system with on-the-move target acquisition and engagement capabilities.

Much like the Avenger system already employed by the US Army, the Crossbow system can fire Stinger ground-to-air antiaircraft missiles.

This up-armored Heavy Hummer prototype is armed with a 30mm automatic cannon in a small turret on top of the vehicle. AM General

An AM General M998 Cargo-Troop Carrier can be modified with various kits to expand mission capability and flexibility. This vehicle features the lightweight weapon-station kit fitted with a 30mm automatic cannon, and the spare-tire and Jerry-can-carrier kits fitted at the rear of the vehicle. AM General

The Crossbow is a pedestal-mounted weapon system (PMWS) designed, built and tested by the Missiles Division of LTV Missiles and Electronics Group. Flexible modularity is the primary objective for the lightweight unit, which can use a variety of platforms and weapons. LTV

The Crossbow pedestal, which can be mounted on trucks, wheeled and tracked personnel carriers or patrol craft, can support several different weapons in ready-to-fire status. It can elevate from minus-ten degrees to plus-seventy-five degrees and has an unrestricted 360 degree azimuth traverse with user-designated no-fire sectors. LTV

What makes this system more advanced is that it can be fitted with a wide variety of both antiaircraft and antitank missiles in single or combination mounts. It also employs a Forward Looking Infrared Field System and a laser range finder. The Crossbow system has already completed extensive testing and is ready for production if ordered.

Hummer Truck

AM General is currently developing and testing a three-person cab-over Hummer truck. It will be offered in

The modular design of Crossbow accommodates a mix of weapons and sensors up to 1,500 pounds. Test firings of .30cal and .50cal machine guns, Spike and HYDRA-70 rockets, the RBS 70 Hellfire, basic and POST versions of Stinger, and the M242 25mm gun prove the pedestal's adaptability and versatility. Configurations for ground combat or naval surface warfare are available. This Crossbow system based on a Hummer is firing a Hellfire missile. LTV

different configurations, including low-bed cargo and flat-bed drop-side cargo. Both cargo beds accommodate troop seats or shelters. The low-bed configuration also accepts the Brunswick Defense BCOE-110 Shelter built specifically for

Designed for the gunner, Crossbow's fire-control console adjusts to every eye-to-monitor position. The gripstick can be mounted where it is most convenient for the gunner. Many of the easy-to-learn controls are automated, as are the decisions for target lead and superelevation. An automatic tracking feature acquires and tracks the target while the gunner identifies the target and its range, selects the weapon and fires. This Hummer-mounted Crossbow system is firing a HYDRA-70 2.75 inch rocket. LTV

this variant. Each configuration incorporates a transfer case with a power take-off (PTO). A high-bed cargo truck has completed over 20,000 miles of independent durability and performance testing. A low-bed cargo carrier is undergoing another 20,000 mile durability test.

The three-person cab-over Hummer truck embodies many of the same components and features as the Heavy Hummer.

Robot Hummer

The US Army and Carnegie-Mellon University in Pittsburgh, Pennsylvania,

The US Army and AM General have worked on numerous ideas and prototypes to improve the Hummer. Not all of them are accepted into service. Shown at the NTC is a prototype armored squad carrier that was designed to carry a fully equipped squad (ten people). US Army

have developed an experimental robot Hummer that can travel at high speed without any human control.

The aim of this Army project is to develop artificial intelligence that would allow robotic military vehicles to "think" as people do and perform high-risk battlefield tasks now done by soldiers.

The robot Hummer is basically a Maxi Ambulance chassis that has been modified to operate as an autonomous road-following vehicle. It is equipped with computer-controlled actuators that control acceleration, braking and steering.

In operation, on-board cameras view the scene ahead of the vehicle and feed the images into a computer. The computer then analyzes these images to

The Hummer prototype armored squad carrier with field packs attached to the rear doors. US Army

The three-person prototype Hummer truck being developed by AM General. AM General

73

find the edges of the road and automatically generates the appropriate driving commands that allow the vehicle to follow a road and avoid obstacles. In the near future, a more sophisticated sensor package that would provide laser and infrared data will make night driving possible by robot Hummer.

A Hummer prototype Armament Carrier fitted with a remote control electric drive turret.

The weapon is the M242 25mm automatic cannon. Department of Defense

Chapter 5

Civilian Hummers

Well-known actor Arnold Schwarzenegger was so impressed with video footage of Hummers in use during Operation Desert Shield and Operation Desert Storm that he contacted the manufacturers of the Hummer and managed to

AM General's first civilian Hummers are scheduled to begin production in June 1992. The civilian Hummers will retain the same drivetrain, chassis and basic body construction as the military version, with certain modifications to fit civilian requirements. AM General

Civilian Hummers will have improved seating and interior appointments, including a lot of soundproofing material that the military versions do not have. AM General

talk them into selling him a custom-built vehicle. Unlike the military version of the Hummer, which has a diesel engine, Schwarzenegger's vehicle has a gasoline engine.

At the strong urging of Schwarzenegger, who convinced the builders of the Hummer that a civilian market for the vehicle existed, AM General announced to the press in late June 1991 that it will produce commercial versions of its Hummer for civilian use.

AM General began taking orders late in 1991. Vehicles are to be delivered in late 1992.

Initially, AM General will market four commercial models of the Hummer: a four-passenger hard-top, a two-door pickup, a four-door pickup and an open-

top sport model. Prices will range from $40,000 to $50,000. Base price for the US government is about $28,000.

The commercial Hummer will feature the same drivetrain, chassis, engine and basic body as the military version. However, it will feature a twelve-volt electrical system, unlike the military's standard twenty-four-volt system, making it compatible with other commercial electrical systems.

Exterior lighting and markings will also be changed to comply with federal standards, and the commercial models will feature more comfortable seating than their military counterparts.

Four primary design changes are required to meet federal safety standards. First, interior occupant protec-

The civilian Hummers will come in four body configurations; four-passenger hardtop, two-door hardtop (as pictured), four-passenger *open-canvas top and a four-passenger enclosed utility vehicle.* AM General

Each civilian Hummer will come with a three-year, 36,000 mile bumper-to-bumper warranty. Also included in the purchase price of a *civilian Hummer will be a tour of AM General's Hummer manufacturing facility and a special one-day training session. AM General*

tion will be added, including a padded instrument panel and interior padded door panels. Second, commercial Hummers will feature steel doors for improved side impact protection. Third, new door locks and latches will add to the vehicle's security. And fourth, the two- and four-door pickup models will feature new hard-tops, replacing the ballistic hard-tops found on military vehicles.

To promote sales to individual customers, the company will initially offer a limited edition of 1,000 vehicles. These first vehicles will be different from all the vehicles that follow, and an identification plate engraved with the vehicle's serial number and the customer's name will be mounted on each limited edition Hummer.

AM General also reached an agreement with the well-known Dallas-based department store chain Neiman-Marcus to sell special edition Hummers through their 1991 Christmas catalog. Unlike the commercial versions sold through AM General, the Neiman-Marcus Hummers will be available with additional features like air conditioning and stereos. They will also come in different colors including red and white.

Besides selling civilian Hummers to individuals, the biggest potential market for nonmilitary variants of the Hummer will be foreign and domestic government agencies. In the United States, the Border Patrol, National Park Service and Forest Service have all begun testing nonmilitary variants of the Hummer.

Civilian Hummers will be equipped with AM/FM stereo radio with cassette player, *Halogen headlamps, three-point seatbelts, and individual bucket seats.* AM General

While the Border Patrol and the National Park Service are mainly looking for a patrol vehicle to replace their fleets of aging jeep-like vehicles, the Forest Service is looking to the Hummer as a state-of-the-art fire-fighting vehicle. Equipped with large storage tanks to carry flame retardant material, and spray nozzles located at the front of the vehicle, the Hummer could go places that are unreachable by the Forest Service's current fleet of wheeled fire-fighting vehicles. Besides the Forest Service, many other fire departments around the country are taking a serious look at the outstanding mobility and load-carrying capability of the Hummer.

Airports around the world depend on modified civilian fire trucks to aid in fighting fires that may result from airplane accidents. Unfortunately, if an airplane accident does not occur on a paved section of the airport and its runways,

Other factory options available for the civilian Hummer include air conditioning, 120 amp alternator, trailer towing package, swingaway spare tire carrier with wheel and tire, 12,000 pound electric winch, underbody protection package, and a brush and headlight guard. AM General

Like the US Army, civilian buyers of the Hummer will also have the chance to buy the AM General Central Tire Inflation System, which gives the Hummer driver control of the *inflation pressure from his dashboard, allowing him on-the-move adjustments to improve traction and adjust the ride characteristics of the vehicle.* AM General

A three-quarter front view of a Red Chinese Hummer. An air-conditioning unit is located on top of the vehicle's roof. AM General

current fire-fighting and rescue vehicles may have great difficulty reaching the crash site. Specially modified Hummers could travel cross-country to reach the crash scene in a fraction of the time needed by current road-bound vehicles.

Besides US government agencies' interest in the Hummer, other countries are looking to the Hummer as an answer to many mobility problems.

Strangely enough, the first foreign government agency to buy nonmilitary variants of the Hummer was Red China. The Chinese Ministry of Petroleum Industry ordered five specially designed Hummers as oil exploration command and support vehicles.

The Chinese Hummers were equipped with a new upper body style, heavy-duty bumpers, special sound and dust insulation, commercial-style bucket seats and steering wheel, air conditioning, AM/FM radio, swing-back spare tire, a sporty paint job and a central tire inflation system. The Hummer was selected by the Chinese because of its rugged construction and ability to operate in wilderness terrain where other vehicles cannot go.

While the Chinese government has been very pleased with the performance of their Hummers and have expressed

A Hummer prototype civilian vehicle used during the 1990 London to Peking Motor Challenge. AM General

interest in acquiring a large number of them both for civilian and military use, the current state of poor relations between the United States and China has stopped any talk of future fleets of Chinese Hummers being placed into service.

Motor Challenge Hummers

AM General also developed two modified civilian Hummers that were entered into the grueling fifty-six-day London to Peking Motor Challenge, organized by the Jules Verne Society in 1990. The company used two M1038 prototype Hummers fitted with a large number of civilian modifications. The biggest change was the substitution of a General Motors gasoline engine in place of the diesel engine found on the standard military models. The vehicles also had larger fuel tanks and a twelve-volt battery system, plus a host of other civilian features like seatbelts and commercial seats. Additional items fitted to them were a portable satellite communications system and a ground positioning system. These Hummers easily mastered all the various road conditions encountered, adding to the long list of Hummer accomplishments.

Appendix

Hummer Specifications

The diagrams and specifications in this appendix are reprinted courtesy of AM General.

ENGINE

SPECIFICATIONS	ENGLISH	METRIC
Type	V8 6.2L	V8 6.2L
Governor Type	Mechanical	
Displacement	379.4 cu. in.	6.2L
Bore & Stroke	3.98 x 3.82 in.	10.0 x 9.7 cm.
Compression Ratio	21.3:1	
Fuel System	Fuel Injection	
Fuel	Diesel	
Fuel Capacity	25.0 gal.	94.6L
Horsepower:	150HP	112 kw.
Gross @ 3,600 RPM	150SAE	112 kw.
Torque Gross @ 2,000 RPM	250 lb.-ft.	339 N-m
Crankcase Cap. w/Filter	8 qts.	7.5L
Cooling System Capacity	26 qts.	24.6L

TRANSMISSION

Type	Automatic	
No. of Speeds: Forward	3	
Reverse	1	
Input Torque Rating	451 lb.-ft.	612 N-m
Ratios: 1st gear	2.48:1	
2nd gear	1.48:1	
3rd gear	1.0:1	
Reverse	2.08:1	
Lubricant Capacity	13.6 qts.	12.87L
Lubricant Type	Dexron II	

TRANS CASE

Type	Full Time Two Speed	
Ratios: Low	2.61:1	
High	1.0:1	
Lubricant Capacity	7 pints	3.3L

AXLES

Front/Rear	Hypoid	
Ratio	2.56:1	
Input Torque Rating	1600 lb.-ft.	2169 N-m
Lubricant Capacity	2 qts.	1.89L

FRAME

Type: Section	Steel Box
No. of Crossmembers	5

BODY

Base Body	Aluminum

ELECTRICAL

Waterproofing	Yes
Radio Suppressed	Yes
Potential Starting	24 V System
Lighting & Accessories	24 V System
Alternator: Rating Amp	60, 100, 200
No. of Batteries	2 - 12 V (In Series)

STEERING

Type	Power Assist	
Ratio Variable	13/16:1	
Lubricant Capacity	1.0 qt.	.45L

BRAKES

Service Brakes Type	Inboard Power Disc w/Dual Master Cylinder	
Actuation	Hydraulic	
Rotor Size	10.5 in. Dia.	266 mm. Dia.
Effective Area: Front	17.4 sq. in.	112.26 sq. cm.
Rear	17.4 sq. in.	112.26 sq. cm.
Parking Brake	Integral w/Rear Service Brakes	
Actuation	Hand Operated Rod & Cable	

SUSPENSION

Type	Independent Dbl. A-frame
Spring: Type	Coil Open End
Shock Absorbers: Type	Hydraulic
Mounting	Upper & Lower Loop
Size	1.75 in. (4.45 cm.) Dia. Piston

TIRES

Type: Non-directional Bias Ply	All Terrain
Size	36 x 12.50-16.5
Run Flat Capability	30 Miles @ 30 MPH

TRANSPORTABILITY

Type of Aircraft:	No. of HUMMERS:
C-130	3
C-141 B	6
C-5 A	15
CH-47	2 (slung under)
CH-53	2 (slung under)
UH-60	1 (slung under)

DEPLOYABILITY

Conventional Air-Drop	All, Except M997; M1037 & M1042 (w/shelters installed)
Low Altitude Parachute Extraction System (LAPES)	

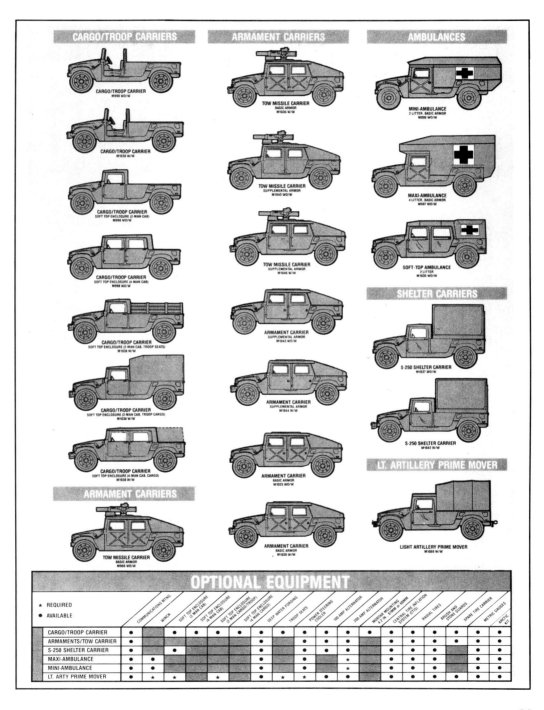

	COMMUNICATIONS MTNG.	WINCH	SOFT TOP ENCLOSURE (2-MAN CAB)	SOFT TOP ENCLOSURE (4-MAN CAB)	SOFT TOP ENCLOSURE (2-MAN CAB, CARGO/TROOP)	SOFT TOP ENCLOSURE (4-MAN CAB)	DEEP WATER FORDING	TROOP SEATS	POWER STEERING COOLER	100 AMP ALTERNATOR	200 AMP ALTERNATOR	MORTAR MOUNTING 4.2 IN. 81MM & 60MM	CENTRAL TIRE INFLATION SYSTEM (CTIS)	RADIAL TIRES	BRUSH AND STONE GUARDS	SPARE TIRE CARRIER	METRIC GAUGES	ARCTIC KIT
CARGO/TROOP CARRIER	●		●	●	●	●		●	●	●	●		●	●	●	●	●	●
ARMAMENTS/TOW CARRIER	●			●	●			●	●	●	●	●	●	●	●	●	●	●
S-250 SHELTER CARRIER	●		●					●	●	●	●		●	●		●	●	●
MAXI-AMBULANCE	●	●						●	●	●	★		●	●	●	●	●	●
MINI-AMBULANCE	●							●	●	●	★		●	●	●	●	●	●
LT. ARTY PRIME MOVER	●	★	★		★		●	★	★	●	●		●	●	●	●	●	●

★ REQUIRED   ● AVAILABLE

OPTIONAL EQUIPMENT

83

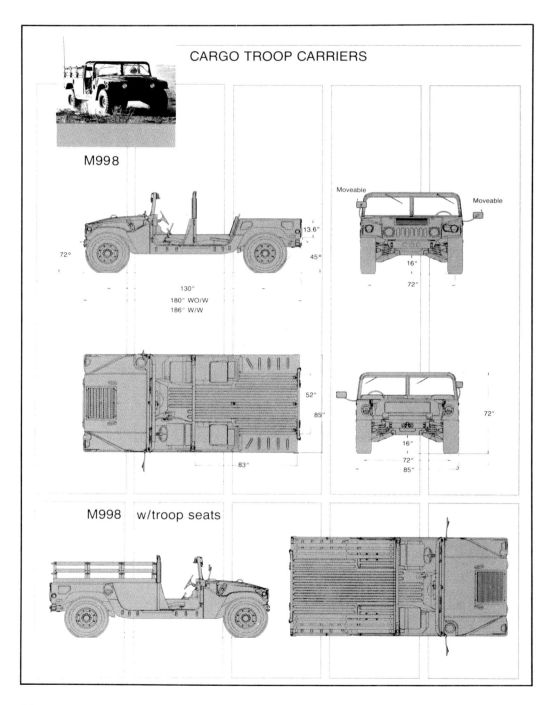

CARGO TROOP CARRIERS

M998

13.6"

72°

45°

130"
180" WO/W
186" W/W

Moveable

Moveable

16"

72"

52"

85"

72"

83"

16"

72"
85"

M998 w/troop seats

M998
CARGO TROOP CARRIER
WO/W

M1038
CARGO TROOP CARRIER
W/W

SPECIFICATIONS	ENGLISH M998/**M1038**	METRIC M998/**M1038**
WEIGHT		
Curb Weight	5,200 lbs./**5,327 lbs.**	2,359 kg./**2,416 kg.**
Payload (See Note 1)	2,500 lbs./**2,373 lbs.**	1,134 kg./**1,077 kg.**
Gross Vehicle Weight (GVW)	7,700 lbs. (both)	3,493 kg. (both)
Gross Axle Weight: Front	3,350 lbs./**3,400 lbs.**	1,520 kg./**1,542 kg.**
Rear	4,350 lbs./**4,300 lbs.**	1,973 kg./**1,950 kg.**
DIMENSIONS AT GVW		
Overall Length	180 in./**186 in.**	4.58 m./**4.72 m.**
Width (w/o mirrors)	85 in. (both)	2.16 m. (both)
Overall Height	72 in. (both)	1.83 m. (both)
Min. Reducible Height*	54 in. (both)	1.37 m. (both)
Min. Ground Clearance	16 in. (both)	0.41 m. (both)
Turning Radius (curb to curb)	24 ft. 4 in. (both)	7.42 m. (both)
Angle of Approach	72°/**47°**	72°/**47°**
Angle of Departure	45° (both)	45° (both)
Shipping Cube	478 cu. ft./**494 cu. ft.**	13.39 cu. m./**13.83 cu. m.**
Wheelbase	130 in. (both)	3.29 m. (both)
Track	72 in. (both)	1.82 m. (both)
Interior Cargo Area: Length	83 in. (both)	2.11 m. (both)
Maximum Width	83 in. (both)	2.11 m. (both)
Width Between Wheelhouses	52 in. (both)	1.31 m. (both)
Depth	13.6 in. (both)	0.35 m. (both)
PERFORMANCE AT GVW		
Speed	65 mph + (both)	105 kmph + (both)
Acceleration: 0 to 30 mph (48 kmph)	8 sec. (both)	8 sec. (both)
0 to 50 mph (80 kmph)	24 sec. (both)	24 sec. (both)
Maximum Towed Load**	3,400 lbs. (both)	1,542 kg. (both)
Grade Capability	60% + (both)	60% + (both)
Side Slope Capability	40% + (both)	40% + (both)
Cruising Range	300 mi. (both)	482 km. (both)
Water Fording Capability:	30 in. (both)	0.76 m. (both)
with Deep Water Fording Kit	60 in. (both)	1.52 m. (both)

GVW — Gross Vehicle Weight.
*Remove soft top and "B" Pillar, and fold windshield.
**Weight at trailer axle.
NOTE 1: Payload includes crew, personal gear, BII (Basic Issue Items), and special kits and equipment. This applies to the payload of entire M998 Series.

W/W — with winch
WO/W — without winch

ARMAMENT CARRIERS

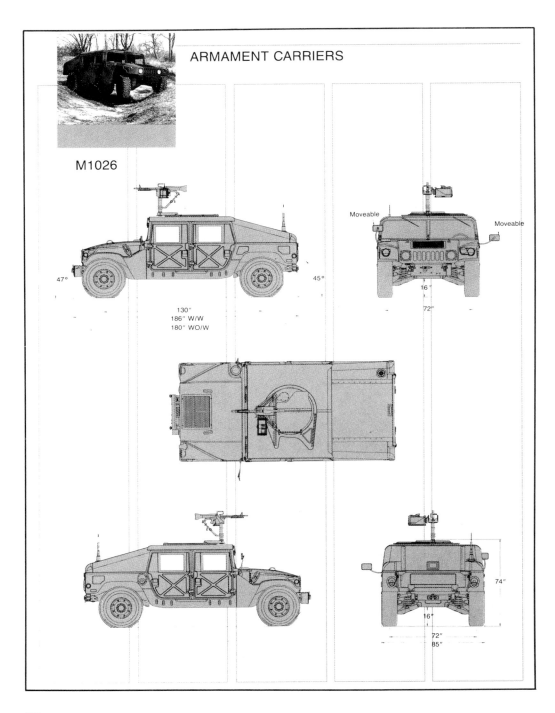

M1026

47°   45°

130"
186" W/W
180" WO/W

Moveable   Moveable

16"
72"

74"

16"
72"
85"

M1025
ARMAMENT CARRIER
BASIC ARMOR   WO/W

M1026
ARMAMENT CARRIER
BASIC ARMOR   W/W

SPECIFICATIONS	ENGLISH M1025/**M1026**	METRIC M1025/**M1026**
WEIGHT		
Curb Weight	5,960 lbs./**6,087 lbs.**	2,703 kg./**2,761 kg.**
Payload	2,240 lbs./**2,113 lbs.**	1,016 kg./**958 kg.**
Gross Vehicle Weight (GVW)	8,200 lbs. (both)	3,720 kg. (both)
Gross Axle Weight: Front	3,685 lbs./**3,840 lbs.**	1,671 kg./**1,742 kg.**
Rear	4,515 lbs./**4,360 lbs.**	2,048 kg./**1,978 kg.**
DIMENSIONS AT GVW		
Overall Length	180 in./**186 in.**	4.58 m./**4.72 m.**
Width (w/o mirrors)	85 in. (both)	2.16 m. (both)
Overall Height (w/o weapon system)	74 in. (both)	1.88 m. (both)
Min. Reducible Height*	72 in. (both)	1.83 m. (both)
Min. Ground Clearance	16 in. (both)	0.41 m. (both)
Turning Radius (curb to curb)	24 ft. 4 in. (both)	7.42 m. (both)
Angle of Approach	72°/**47°**	72°/**47°**
Angle of Departure	45° (both)	45° (both)
Shipping Cube	638 cu. ft./**659 cu. ft.**	17.85 cu. m./**18.45 cu. m.**
Wheelbase	130 in. (both)	3.29 m. (both)
Track	72 in. (both)	1.82 m. (both)
Interior Cargo Area: Length	83 in. (both)	2.11 m. (both)
Maximum Width	83 in. (both)	2.11 m. (both)
Width Between Wheelhouses	52 in. (both)	1.31 m. (both)
PERFORMANCE AT GVW		
Speed	65 mph + (both)	105 kmph + (both)
Acceleration: 0 to 30 mph (48 kmph)	8 sec. (both)	8 sec. (both)
0 to 50 mph (80 kmph)	24 sec. (both)	24 sec. (both)
Maximum Towed Load**	3,400 lbs. (both)	1,542 kg. (both)
Grade Capability	60% + (both)	60% + (both)
Side Slope Capability	40% + (both)	40% + (both)
Cruising Range	300 mi. (both)	482 km. (both)
Water Fording Capability:	30 in. (both)	0.76 m. (both)
with Deep Water Fording Kit	60 in. (both)	1.52 m. (both)

GVW — Gross Vehicle Weight.
*Remove armament mount.
**Weight at trailer axle.

W/W — with winch
WO/W — without winch

Appendix

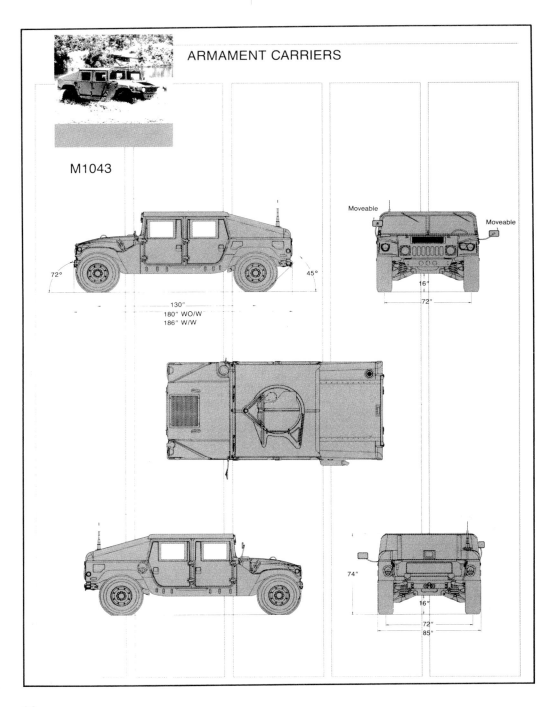

ARMAMENT CARRIERS

M1043

Moveable

Moveable

72°

45°

16"

72"

130"
180" WO/W
186" W/W

74"

16"

72"
85"

M1043
ARMAMENT CARRIER
SUPPLEMENTAL ARMOR   WO/W

M1044
ARMAMENT CARRIER
SUPPLEMENTAL ARMOR   W/W

SPECIFICATIONS	ENGLISH M1043/**M1044**	METRIC M1043/**M1044**
Curb Weight	6,411 lbs./**6,538 lbs.**	2,908 kg./**2,966 kg.**
Payload	1,989 lbs./**1,862 lbs.**	902 kg./**845 kg.**
Gross Vehicle Weight (GVW)	8,400 lbs. (both)	3,810 kg. (both)
Gross Axle Weight: Front	3,961 lbs./**4,092 lbs.**	1,797 kg./**1,856 kg.**
Rear	4,439 lbs./**4,308 lbs.**	2,014 kg./**1,954 kg.**
Overall Length	180 in./**186 in.**	4.58 m./**4.72 m.**
Width (w/o mirrors)	85 in. (both)	2.16 m. (both)
Overall Height (w/o weapon system)	74 in. (both)	1.88 m. (both)
Min. Reducible Height*	72 in. (both)	1.83 m. (both)
Min. Ground Clearance	16 in. (both)	0.41 m. (both)
Turning Radius (curb to curb)	24 ft. 4 in. (both)	7.42 m. (both)
Angle of Approach	72°/**47°**	72°/**47°**
Angle of Departure	45° (both)	45° (both)
Shipping Cube	638 cu. ft./**659 cu. ft.**	7.85 cu. m./**18.45 cu. m.**
Wheelbase	130 in. (both)	3.29 m. (both)
Track	72 in. (both)	1.82 m. (both)
Interior Cargo Area: Length	83 in. (both)	2.11 m. (both)
Maximum Width	83 in. (both)	2.11 m. (both)
Width Between Wheelhouses	52 in. (both)	1.31 m. (both)
Speed	65 mph + (both)	105 kmph + (both)
Acceleration: 0 to 30 mph (48 kmph)	8 sec. (both)	8 sec. (both)
0 to 50 mph (80 kmph)	24 sec. (both)	24 sec. (both)
Maximum Towed Load**	3,400 lbs. (both)	1,542 kg. (both)
Grade Capability	60% + (both)	60% + (both)
Side Slope Capability	40% + (both)	40% + (both)
Cruising Range	300 mi. (both)	482 km. (both)
Water Fording Capability:	30 in. (both)	0.76 m. (both)
with Deep Water Fording Kit	60 in. (both)	1.52 m. (both)

GVW — Gross Vehicle Weight.
*Remove armament mount.
**Weight at trailer axle.

W/W — with winch
WO/W — without winch

TOW MISSILE CARRIERS

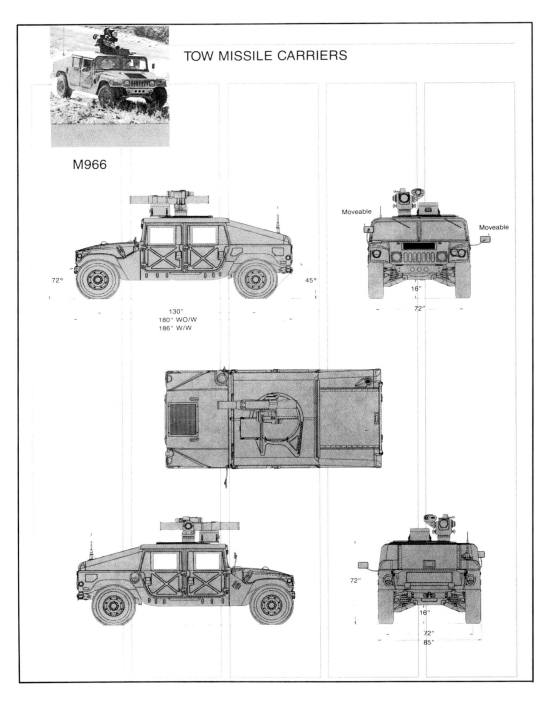

M966

72°   45°

130"
180" WO/W
186" W/W

Moveable

Moveable

16"

72"

72"

16"

72"

85"

M966
TOW MISSILE CARRIER
BASIC ARMOR   WO/W

M1036
TOW MISSILE CARRIER
BASIC ARMOR   **W/W**

SPECIFICATIONS	ENGLISH M966/**M1036**	METRIC M966/**M1036**
WEIGHT		
Curb Weight	6,051 lbs./**6,178 lbs.**	2,745 kg./**2,802 kg.**
Payload	2,149 lbs./**2,022 lbs.**	975 kg./**917 kg.**
Gross Vehicle Weight (GVW)	8,200 lbs. (both)	3,719 kg. (both)
Gross Axle Weight: Front	3,550 lbs./**3,700 lbs.**	1,610 kg./**1,678 kg.**
Rear	4,650 lbs./**4,500 lbs.**	2,068 kg./**2,041 kg.**
DIMENSIONS AT GVW		
Overall Length	180 in./**186 in.**	4.58 m./**4.72 m.**
Width (w/o mirrors)	85 in. (both)	2.16 m. (both)
Overall Height (w/o TOW)	72 in. (both)	1.83 m. (both)
Min. Reducible Height	72 in. (both)	1.83 m. (both)
Min. Ground Clearance	16 in. (both)	0.41 m. (both)
Turning Radius (curb to curb)	24 ft. 4 in. (both)	7.42 m. (both)
Angle of Approach	72°/**47°**	72°/**47°**
Angle of Departure	45° (both)	45° (both)
Shipping Cube	638 cu. ft./**659 cu. ft.**	17.85 cu. m./**18.45 cu. m.**
Wheelbase	130 in. (both)	3.29 m. (both)
Track	72 in. (both)	1.82 m. (both)
Interior Cargo Area: Length	83 in. (both)	2.11 m. (both)
Maximum Width	83 in. (both)	2.11 m. (both)
Width Between Wheelhouses	52 in. (both)	1.31 m. (both)
PERFORMANCE AT GVW		
Speed	65 mph + (both)	105 kmph + (both)
Acceleration: 0 to 30 mph (48 kmph)	8 sec. (both)	8 sec. (both)
0 to 50 mph (80 kmph)	24 sec. (both)	24 sec. (both)
Maximum Towed Load*	3,400 lbs. (both)	1,542 kg. (both)
Grade Capability	60% + (both)	60% + (both)
Side Slope Capability	40% + (both)	40% + (both)
Cruising Range	300 mi. (both)	482 km. (both)
Water Fording Capability:	30 in. (both)	0.76 m. (both)
with Deep Water Fording Kit	60 in. (both)	1.52 m. (both)

GVW — Gross Vehicle Weight.
*Weight at trailer axle.

W/W — with winch
WO/W — without winch

91

Appendix

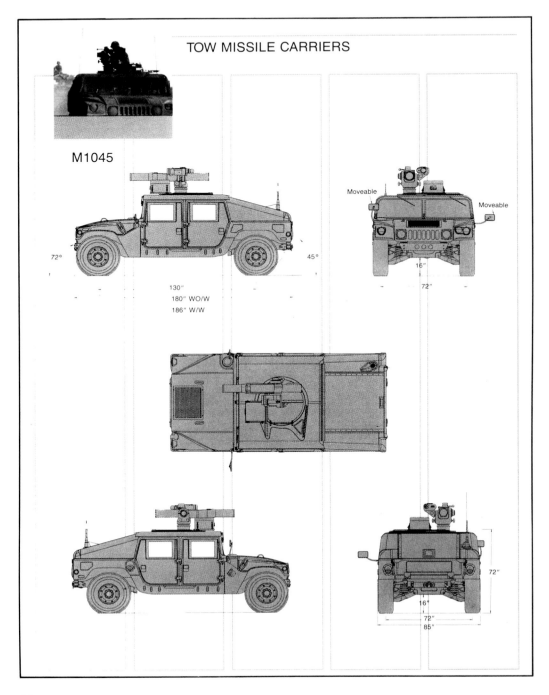

TOW MISSILE CARRIERS

M1045

72°   45°

130"
180" WO/W
186" W/W

Moveable   Moveable

16"
72"

72"

16"
72"
85"

92

M1045
TOW MISSILE CARRIER
SUPPLEMENTAL ARMOR   WO/W

M1046
TOW MISSILE CARRIER
SUPPLEMENTAL ARMOR   W/W

	SPECIFICATIONS	ENGLISH M1045/**M1046**	METRIC M1045/**M1046**
WEIGHT	Curb Weight	6,438 lbs./**6,565 lbs.**	2,920 kg./**2,978 kg.**
	Payload	1,962 lbs./**1,835 lbs.**	890 kg./**832 kg.**
	Gross Vehicle Weight (GVW)	8,400 lbs. (both)	3,810 kg. (both)
	Gross Axle Weight: Front	3,725 lbs./**3,850 lbs.**	1,690 kg./**1,746 kg.**
	Rear	4,675 lbs./**4,550 lbs.**	2,121 kg./**2,064 kg.**
DIMENSIONS AT GVW	Overall Length	180 in./**186 in.**	4.58 m./**4.72 m.**
	Width (w/o mirrors)	85 in. (both)	2.16 m. (both)
	Overall Height (w/o TOW)	72 in. (both)	1.83 m. (both)
	Min. Reducible Height	72 in. (both)	1.83 m. (both)
	Min. Ground Clearance	16 in. (both)	0.41 m. (both)
	Turning Radius (curb to curb)	24 ft. 4 in. (both)	7.42 m. (both)
	Angle of Approach	72°/**47°**	72°/**47°**
	Angle of Departure	45° (both)	45° (both)
	Shipping Cube	638 cu. ft./**659 cu. ft.**	17.85 cu. m./**18.45 cu. m.**
	Wheelbase	130 in. (both)	3.29 m. (both)
	Track	72 in. (both)	1.82 m. (both)
	Interior Cargo Area: Length	83 in. (both)	2.11 m. (both)
	Maximum Width	83 in. (both)	2.11 m. (both)
	Width Between Wheelhouses	52 in. (both)	1.31 m. (both)
PERFORMANCE AT GVW	Speed	65 mph + (both)	105 kmph + (both)
	Acceleration: 0 to 30 mph (48 kmph)	8 sec. (both)	8 sec. (both)
	0 to 50 mph (80 kmph)	24 sec. (both)	24 sec. (both)
	Maximum Towed Load*	3,400 lbs. (both)	1,542 kg. (both)
	Grade Capability	60% + (both)	60% + (both)
	Side Slope Capability	40% + (both)	40% + (both)
	Cruising Range	300 mi. (both)	482 km. (both)
	Water Fording Capability:	30 in. (both)	0.76 m. (both)
	with Deep Water Fording Kit	60 in. (both)	1.52 m. (both)

GVW — Gross Vehicle Weight.
*Weight at trailer axle.

W/W — with winch
WO/W — without winch

Appendix

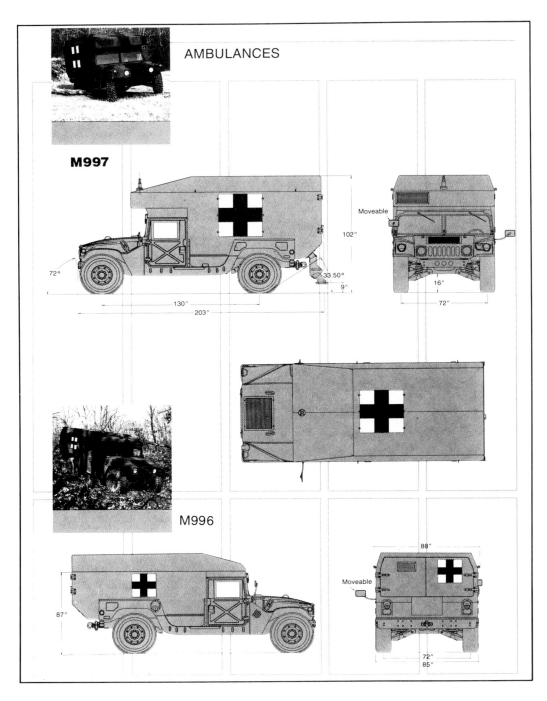

AMBULANCES

M997

Moveable

102"

72°   33.50°

9"

16"

72"

130"

203"

M996

88"

Moveable

87"

72"

85"

94

M996
MINI-AMBULANCE BASIC ARMOR
2-LITTER OR 6 AMBULATORY PATIENTS   WO/W

M997
MAXI-AMBULANCE BASIC ARMOR
4-LITTER OR 8 AMBULATORY PATIENTS   WO/W

SPECIFICATIONS	ENGLISH M996/**M997**	METRIC M996/**M997**
WEIGHT		
Curb Weight	6,748 lbs./**7,180 lbs.**	3,061 kg./**3,257 kg.**
Payload	1,912 lbs./**1,920 lbs.**	867 kg./**871 kg.**
Gross Vehicle Weight (GVW)	8,660 lbs./**9,100 lbs.**	3,928 kg./**4,128 kg.**
Gross Axle Weight: Front	3,673 lbs./**3,860 lbs.**	1,666 kg./**1,751 kg.**
Rear	4,987 lbs./**5,240 lbs.**	2,262 kg./**2,377 kg.**
DIMENSIONS AT GVW		
Overall Length	203 in. (both)	5.2 m.(both)
Width (w/o mirrors)	85 in. (both)	2.16 m. (both)
Overall Height*	87 in./**102 in.**	2.21 m./**2.59 m.**
Min. Reducible Height	Not applicable	Not applicable
Min. Ground Clearance	16 in. (both)	0.41 m. (both)
Turning Radius (curb to curb)	24 ft. 4 in. (both)	7.42 m. (both)
Angle of Approach	72° (both)	72° (both)
Angle of Departure	33.50° (both)	33.50° (both)
Shipping Cube	869 cu. ft./**1,019 cu. ft.**	24.33 cu.m./**28.51 cu.m.**
Wheelbase	130 in. (both)	3.29 m. (both)
Track	72 in. (both)	1.82 m. (both)
Interior Patient Area: Length	104 in. (both)	2.64 m. (both)
Maximum Width	82 in. (both)	2.06 m. (both)
Width Between Wheelhouses	48 in. (both)	1.22 m. (both)
Height	49 in./64 in.	1.24 in./1.63 in.
PERFORMANCE AT GVW		
Speed	65 mph + (both)	105 kmph + (both)
Acceleration: 0 to 30 mph (48 kmph)	8 sec./**9.1 sec.**	8 sec./**9.1 sec.**
0 to 50 mph (80 kmph)	24 sec./**26 sec.**	24 sec./**26 sec.**
Maximum Towed Load**	3,400 lbs. (both)	1,542 kg. (both)
Grade Capability	60% + (both)	60% + (both)
Side Slope Capability	40% + (both)	40% + (both)
Cruising Range	275 mi. (both)	445 km. (both)
Water Fording Capability:	30 in. (both)	0.76 m. (both)
with Deep Water Fording Kit	60 in. (both)	1.52 m. (both)

*Overall height is curb weight (unloaded)
**Weight at trailer axle.

GVW — Gross Vehicle Weight.
WO/W — without winch.

Index